IMAGES
of America

OREGON'S
COVERED BRIDGES

Cows are herded across the Bates Park Covered Bridge in Linn County in 1956. This two-span bridge crossed the South Santiam River near Lebanon. Built in 1921 and replaced in 1957, the older red span was 139 feet 6 inches long. The 153-foot-8-inch white span was built in 1930 and replaced in 1970. (Courtesy Salem Public Library Historic Photograph Collection.)

ON THE COVER: The Ritner Creek Bridge in Polk County provided an excellent spot for these young ladies to sell worms, cookies, and soft drinks during opening day of fishing season in 1959. Ritner Creek Bridge was constructed in 1927 at a cost of less than $7,000. When it was replaced with a concrete bridge in 1976, the covered bridge was the last one to span a creek on a state highway. It looked very similar to the Kings Valley Bridge, just a few miles away in Benton County. (Courtesy Salem Public Library Historic Photograph Collection.)

IMAGES
of America

OREGON'S COVERED BRIDGES

Bill Cockrell

ARCADIA
PUBLISHING

Published by Arcadia Publishing
Charleston, South Carolina

Library of Congress Catalog Card Number: 2007940258

For all general information contact Arcadia Publishing at:
Telephone 843-853-2070
Fax 843-853-0044
E-mail sales@arcadiapublishing.com
For customer service and orders:
Toll-Free 1-888-313-2665

Visit us on the Internet at www.arcadiapublishing.com

To the early bridge builders who helped to span the wild streams of Oregon's Willamette Valley. And to the late Fred Kildow, who inspired me to start the covered bridge research.

CONTENTS

ACKNOWLEDGMENTS

Special thanks go to the Oregon Department of Transportation (ODOT) for providing access to historic photographs and negatives, along with microfilmed records that documented the history and folklore of the old wooden covered bridges. The author is indebted to the Salem Public Library's Historic Photograph Collection, which supplied visual record of Oregon's covered bridges from the 1930s through the 1950s. The Fred Kildow collection was a great treasure of long-gone covered bridges. Special thanks go to Chris Leedham, who provided valuable assistance in organizing this volume. A large debt of gratitude goes to Stevie Convey for valuable proofreading assistance. Finally, thanks go to Joseph Conwill, who encouraged the completion of this book.

INTRODUCTION

These narratives and photographs tell how early bridge builders struggled to overcome the frontier environment in Oregon. More than 600 covered bridge sites once dotted the state's landscape. Today only 50 of these wooden structures exist.

Early builders used the Smith truss, one imported from the states east of the Mississippi River. No covered bridge remains in Oregon today of this type. Later the Howe truss soon became the mechanism for most of Oregon's covered bridges. The 1915 Oregon legislature enacted a law requiring all bridges costing $500 or more to be built under the supervision of the Oregon State Highway Department. The department soon developed standard Howe truss plans for counties to use. Today all but a few covered bridges use this truss. The Howe truss is one of the easiest for unskilled workers to assemble, as it is a series of Xs with vertical iron rods. The queenpost and kingpost trusses were widely used as well, especially on shorter covered spans. One kingpost truss covered bridge, Neal Lane Bridge in Douglas County, exists today and only three queenpost truss bridges span streams in the state.

In the 1940s and 1950s, counties often considered covered bridges as impediments to modern vehicular traffic, and so many were replaced. Loaded logging trucks needed bridges with no height restrictions. Many examples of this practice are evident in photographs of splintered portal boards. Ironically, counties continued to build covered bridges into the 1950s and even into the 1960s. The abundance of Douglas fir timber helped convince counties to use this material for bridge construction.

Folklore often colors the reason for covering a bridge. Some people say it was to keep anglers dry, while some say it was to trick horses into thinking the bridge was actually a barn, so they would enter freely. Some even think builders hid their shoddy workmanship with the covering. The actual reason for the covered bridge was to protect the truss from moisture. The uncovered bridge might last eight or nine years, but a covered bridge could last several times that long. The act of constructing sides and a roof was therefore an economic decision.

The future of covered bridges in Oregon seems secure. Counties recognize the emotional appeal these structures evoke. And tourism provides a monetary reason to maintain covered bridges.

At one time, five covered bridges spanned Thomas Creek in Linn County. Pictured here is the Jordan Bridge, about eight miles east of Scio. This 1946 photograph shows the structure with a rounded portal and open sides, the standard design adopted by Linn County during the 1930s and 1940s. The Jordan Bridge was dismantled in 1985 and moved to Stayton in Marion County, where it was reconstructed in a city park. It burned in 1994 but was rebuilt by volunteers in 1998. (Courtesy Salem Public Library Historic Photograph Collection.)

One

BENTON COUNTY

The Flynn Bridge was one of many covered spans designed by the state yet built by the county. In this case, the Benton County bridge crew constructed it in 1922 at a cost of $8,819.43. One of a half-dozen covered bridges to span Marys River, the little Flynn Bridge lasted only until 1948, when it was replaced with a concrete span. Benton County lay midway between the capital city of Salem and the Pacific Ocean. As the population increased, public influence caused the county to take title to the roads and bridges. Benton County financed the maintenance and rebuilding of its bridges, which spanned streams such as Marys River, Alsea River, Long Tom River, and the Luckiamute River. Today only Hayden Bridge, Irish Bend Bridge, and Harris Bridge greet visitors. (Courtesy ODOT.)

A sign commonly seen on heavily traveled roads is "Impaired Clearance." At Benton County's Mill Creek Bridge near Alsea, the vertical clearance at the centerline was just 15 feet. This bridge spanned Mill Creek from 1924 until its replacement in 1953. At that time, it was the last covered bridge on the state's primary road system. (Courtesy ODOT.)

Noon Bridge, pictured here in the 1940s, shows a rounded portal opening. Due to larger truck and bus traffic, the state expanded the openings at each end several years after construction. Benton County workers built the 120-foot Howe truss bridge in 1924. It spanned Marys River between Wren and Philomath until its replacement in the mid-1940s. (Courtesy ODOT.)

Benton County workers constructed this state-designed bridge in 1922 at a cost of $4,066.22. The 75-foot Howe truss structure spanned Marys River three-quarters of a mile north of Wren on the Wren-Kings Valley Highway. For additional lighting, the county installed windows along each side. The bridge was replaced in July 1950. (Courtesy ODOT.)

This 75-foot Howe truss Kings Valley Bridge over the Luckiamute River was a state-designed structure built by Benton County workers in 1924. Much like the nearby Ritner Creek Bridge in Polk County, it contained rounded portal openings and Gothic-style windows on both sides. The Kings Valley Bridge gave way to a concrete bridge in 1965. (Courtesy ODOT.)

Benton County laborers built this 75-foot Howe truss in 1938. Based on costs of materials and labor, the final expenditures totaled $3,815. The Hoskins Bridge spanned the Luckiamute River in the small hamlet of Hoskins until 1963. The 1962 Columbus Day windstorm blew tall fir trees onto the bridge, necessitating its replacement. (Courtesy ODOT.)

This photograph shows the 75-foot Bush Bridge during the construction of its replacement in 1958. Bush Bridge crossed the Luckiamute River just one mile from the Hoskins Bridge. Benton County files show that county employees constructed the covered span in 1936 at a cost of $2,875. (Courtesy Salem Public Library Historic Photograph Collection.)

Details regarding the construction date of the 60-foot Irish Bend Bridge are clouded with confusion. Some records state it was built in 1938, while others show its construction in 1954. Most likely, the bridge was rebuilt in 1954 using the wooden timbers from the 1938 bridge. It spanned a slough near the Willamette River a few miles south of Corvallis. When the author photographed this view in 1976, the bridge had been put up for adoption. Volunteers eventually moved the timbers onto the Oregon State University campus and reconstructed it over Oak Creek in 1989.

Bundy Bridge spanned the Long Tom River a few miles north of Monroe. The 75-foot Howe truss was built in 1939 using county labor. The 1943 inspection report showed it to be in good shape, but the bridge was bypassed with a concrete span in 1961. A few years later, a county crew set fire to the sagging structure, leaving only smoldering embers. (Courtesy ODOT.)

13

Seen here is another of the standard 75-foot Howe truss covered bridges built by Benton County. Stow Pit Road Bridge crossed the Long Tom River from 1939 until its replacement just prior to 1960. The 1943 inspection showed the bridge to be in excellent condition, yet it was still dismantled just a few years later. (Courtesy ODOT.)

The Dodge Slough Bridge (also known as Lemon Creek Bridge) near Monroe is an example of the 75-foot Howe truss spans built in the older Benton County style. The low portal openings restricted load heights. Inspections in the 1940s revealed decay in the abutments, but the stringers on the truss were rated at 85 percent. The inspector noted, "Timber in truss apparently sound. Piers are weakest part of truss." (Courtesy ODOT.)

This 60-foot Howe truss span was located over Marys River just south of Philomath. County workers built the wooden truss Philomath Bridge in 1936. Inspections prior to 1960 showed the bridge to be in excellent shape, but decay eventually weakened the truss members. Benton County built a concrete span in 1963 to bypass the bridge. A local garden club raised funds to preserve it, but the efforts fell far short, and the wooden covered span was removed in 1969. (Courtesy Salem Public Library Historic Photograph Collection.)

In 1938, the two-span roofed Kiger Island Bridge was built for just $9,845 to replace an earlier covered span. At the time of construction, it was the longest in Benton County; each span was 170 feet, for a total length of 340 feet. The bridge spanned Boonesville Channel of the Willamette River, just three miles south of Corvallis. Farmers and merchants often complained about the low clearance of the portal openings. By the late 1950s, the county had decided to replace it with a concrete bridge. At the end of 1963, the old covered span was torn down. (Courtesy ODOT.)

Just two-tenths of a mile from the small community of Wren, the 60-foot Wren Bridge crossed Marys River. Benton County workers built it in 1938 at a cost of $2,950. Just six years later in 1944, the inspection report noted, "Posts for truss very rotten @ bearing on sill." Laborers added windows in the late 1950s because the bridge began at a slight curve in the road. It was replaced in 1967. (Courtesy ODOT.)

The Moody Bridge spanned the Luckiamute River about two miles north of Hoskins near the historic site of Fort Hoskins. County workers constructed the 75-foot covered bridge in 1932. The state supplied bridge plans to the county for its replacement in 1956, but the plans were revised and reissued in 1958. On the right is the pony truss Valley and Siletz Railroad span, built in 1946. (Courtesy ODOT.)

This rail bridge crossed the Luckiamute about two miles north of Hoskins and adjacent to the Moody Bridge. Three of these unroofed but covered trusses were situated along the Valley and Siletz line. This one, an 80-foot pony truss, was built in 1946 and covered in 1947. The rails were removed in the 1960s and 1970s. (Courtesy Kildow collection.)

A 92-foot Howe truss, the rustic Salmonberry Covered Bridge spanned Alsea River several miles west of Alsea beginning in 1938. The 1944 inspection report indicated that the decking, stringers, and piers were at 80 percent. The inspector noted, "Truss probably 20 years old." This suggests that the truss members had been used in a previous bridge or that the Salmonberry Bridge was rebuilt in 1938 using timbers from the older bridge. It was replaced in 1959. (Courtesy ODOT.)

A covered bridge has passed over the Alsea River at this spot since 1918. The 91-foot Howe truss Hayden Covered Bridge, pictured here, was the first. A February 1944 inspection report noted the deteriorated condition of the wooden span. It rated the piers, stringers, decking, and trusses at 50 percent. The inspector stated, "Bridge is to be rebuilt this year. Truss built 1918 according to farmer living at bridge site. Approaches have been replaced more than once." In 1945, the old structure was replaced with the current Hayden Bridge. (Courtesy ODOT.)

Honey Grove Bridge spanned the Alsea River on Honey Grove Road just east of Alsea. The first Honey Grove Covered Bridge was a 96-foot Howe truss built in 1918. It lasted until 1940, when the second bridge, seen here, was built as a seven-panel, 96-foot Howe truss. Construction costs totaled $3,200. Loaded farm trucks and logging trucks often damaged the housing boards above the portal openings. This span was replaced in 1965. (Courtesy ODOT.)

Two

CLACKAMAS AND WASHINGTON COUNTIES

When the Fields Bridge was built in 1925, it replaced an earlier covered span that had lasted from 1873 to 1925. E. D. Olds served as the prime contractor. Construction costs for the 176-foot Howe truss totaled $7,664.83. County workers actually removed some siding boards during a flood to reduce the likelihood that the raging waters would wash the bridge from its piers. The Fields Bridge crossed the Tualatin River for only 28 years and was replaced with a concrete span in 1953. Clackamas and Washington Counties, located in northwest Oregon, have no existing covered bridges. The history of their covered bridge construction began in the mid-1850s, and the flood of 1861 washed most of them away. The Tualatin River flowed through both counties, and each built roofed bridges to span that stream. In Clackamas County, the Molalla River, the Clackamas River, the Sandy River, and the Pudding River hosted covered bridges. The last, the Trout Creek Bridge, was removed in 1954. (Courtesy ODOT.)

Probably the most interesting of the Clackamas County covered bridges is the old Knights Bridge over the Molalla River. Noted bridge builder A. S. Miller constructed the 211-foot two-span bridge in 1877. One span was an 87-foot Howe truss, and the other was a 124-foot modified arch truss. Farmers complained that the portals were too small for truckloads of produce to get to market. Some stated they took wheels off trailers and wagons and pulled them along the bridge deck on their axles. A strong windstorm blew the bridge into the river in 1947. (Courtesy Salem Public Library Historic Photograph Collection.)

This photograph shows the interior of the two-span Knights Bridge. The 1940 inspection report stated, "Lower chord on left side in 124' span quite badly checked; and is cross grained. Some stringers rest only on 2" pieces scabbed to sides of lower chord. This whole structure doesn't look like a very safe affair." (Courtesy ODOT.)

20

Dickie Prairie Bridge was one of the last covered spans on a Clackamas County road system. Here a bread truck travels through the old wooden span. The warning sign states, "One truck at a time on this bridge." E. D. Olds and J. D. Hardy built the 105-foot truss over the Molalla River in 1920 for $5,500. The 1940 inspection report noted that the bridge was in overall good shape but mentioned that lots of heavily loaded logging trucks hauling 60,000 pounds used the bridge. By the early 1950s, the county had restricted the loads, and the bridge was replaced in 1954. (Courtesy ODOT.)

The rustic Red Bridge near the old Pat's Acres Resort spanned the Pudding River until 1954, when the county declared it unsafe for bus and truck traffic. In the interest of safety, school bus drivers unloaded their buses of children before entering the aging structure in 1953 and 1954. The county built the 100-foot Howe truss bridge in 1915 for a tidy sum of $5,000. The cost to remove the bridge was $3,835. (Courtesy ODOT.)

Little is known about the old wooden Glen Avon Bridge, which crossed the Molalla River near Canby. The 71-foot Howe truss was constructed in 1905 and lasted until 1939. It looked very similar to the Trout Creek Bridge, which spanned the Molalla River only a few miles away. Old records show it was known as Bridge No. 6555. (Courtesy ODOT.)

Rhododendron Bridge passed over the Sandy River a short distance from the small community of Zigzag in eastern Clackamas County. The 85-foot Howe truss bridge was constructed in 1915 by an unknown builder. The old span lasted until 1943, when a heavy snowfall caused its collapse. (Courtesy ODOT.)

Trout Creek Bridge was located on a remote road across the Molalla River not far from the Glen Avon Bridge, about six miles from Molalla. The 60-foot span was built in 1928 and lasted only until its replacement in July 1957, a life of 29 years. Its rustic appearance often led visitors to guess its age as much older. Trout Creek Bridge was the last covered span in Clackamas County. (Courtesy ODOT.)

Research into the details of the Eagle Creek Bridge near Eagle Creek reveals that the 100-foot truss was numbered 6561. It was located on Road 1024 at milepost 6.20. Construction and removal dates have not been found, but the date of this photograph is 1903. The trestle on the right was 105 feet high, the tallest of any in the county at the time. (Courtesy Kildow collection.)

The Oregon and California Railroad built this bridge around 1870. It lasted only a few years before it washed away, probably in the flood of 1890–1891. The bridge spanned the Clackamas River near Gladstone. (Courtesy Kildow collection.)

Located in the small community of Monitor near the Marion and Clackamas line, the Monitor Bridge crossed Butte Creek starting sometime between 1900 and 1905. It was replaced with a concrete bridge in 1938. (Courtesy Salem Public Library Historic Photograph Collection.)

A river ferry plied the Clackamas River near Carver until the Baker's Ferry Covered Bridge was constructed in 1883. Peter Paquet and a small crew built the 230-foot Smith truss bridge to replace the old ferry. The wooden span lasted until a replacement steel truss bridge was erected in 1931. (Courtesy Kildow collection.)

E. D. Olds and J. W. Reed constructed the 140-foot Howe truss High Bridge (also known as Estacada Lake Bridge) in 1908. In 1933, Clackamas County agreed to let the Estacada Chamber of Commerce remove the wooden housing for the value of the salvaged lumber. A new concrete bridge was built in 1936. A short time later, workers dynamited the wooden truss. (Courtesy ODOT.)

This photograph shows Estacada's High Bridge just prior to replacement. The siding has already been removed. (Courtesy ODOT.)

Near the small community of Liberal in Clackamas County, Harrison Wright oversaw the construction of a one-span covered bridge across the Molalla River. For a number of years, the bridge, which was built in 1866, operated as a toll. Eventually, the county gave Wright $2,500 to make it free. The Wright Bridge lasted until 1928, when it was replaced with a steel truss span. (Courtesy Kildow collection.)

A short distance east of Carver, the Clear Creek Bridge replaced an earlier covered bridge crossing Clear Creek at the same site. The single-span structure was built in 1884 and lasted until a steel truss bridge was erected in 1912. (Courtesy Kildow collection.)

The 116-foot Sleepy Hollow Bridge spanned the Sandy River just south of Brightwood. The construction date is unknown, but the 1942 inspection report noted that the timbers were sound or were repaired to be 100 percent. The stringers were transverse on top of the bottom chords. The decking was 4 by 12 inches, placed diagonally at 45 degrees with a 4-by-12-inch plank running lengthwise. The bridge housing consisted of 1-by-12-inch boards. Sleepy Hollow Bridge was replaced in 1949. (Courtesy ODOT.)

At Canby, an on-deck Oregon and California Railroad bridge spanned the Molalla River beginning in 1873. It was replaced with an on-deck steel truss bridge in 1907. In 1901, E. D. Olds built the adjacent covered road bridge, which lasted until 1920. His son used some of the timbers to build the Fields Bridge over the Tualatin River. Both bridges were recorded in this photograph around 1910. (Courtesy ODOT.)

This Washington County bridge spanned the Tualatin River about three miles south of Tigard. The State of Oregon built the 144-foot Howe truss in 1918 at a cost of $12,968.60. It featured laminated wood flooring and windows at panel points for increased visibility. After a short life, it gave way to a new concrete span. (Courtesy ODOT.)

The rustic-looking Minter Bridge was located near Hillsboro in Washington County. This 100-foot covered wooden truss span was built over the Tualatin River in 1898 and replaced in the 1930s. (Courtesy ODOT.)

Some three miles northeast of Sandy, the Bull Run Bridge was built around 1900. The 10-panel Howe truss bridge measured about 150 feet long. Construction workers and employees of the electric company were the main residents in this area. (Courtesy Kildow collection.)

Three

CLATSOP, TILLAMOOK, AND YAMHILL COUNTIES

The demand for steel during World War I led the Oregon State Highway Commission to design wooden covered spans in the style of this bridge in Clatsop County near Astoria. Engineers included windows between the truss members and specified that the interior be whitewashed for increased lighting. The 1918 bridge cost about $25,000 and lasted only until 1933, giving just 15 years of service. No covered bridges still stand in these three counties in western Oregon. However, photographs and inspection reports reveal structures rustic in design and sparingly maintained—with one exception: the state-designed John Day River Bridge near Astoria, a one-of-a-kind counterweighted center-lift span. (Courtesy ODOT.)

This view shows the unique and detailed characteristics used in the construction of the John Day River Bridge in Clatsop County. It was one of the first in the state to receive a whitewashed interior, which was used to increase lighting and visibility. (Courtesy ODOT.)

North Fork Beaver Creek Bridge spanned the creek on the Netarts-Sandlake Road at milepost 1.0. Tillamook County workers built the 38-foot truss in 1930, with construction costs totaling $1,200. This photograph, taken by the bridge inspector, shows that high loads have knocked portal boards from the bridge end. The date of replacement is unknown. (Courtesy ODOT.)

The Dougherty Slough Bridge crossed the slough near Beaver on the Wilson Loop Road at milepost 0.9. Tillamook County constructed the 70-foot Howe truss bridge in 1918 for $2,800. In 1951, the old span was replaced with a 156-foot reinforced concrete bridge. (Courtesy ODOT.)

The two-span Ollie Woods Bridge passed over the Big Nestucca River near Beaver. Each span was a 100-foot Howe truss. The wooden structure cost the county $5,500 to construct in 1921. In later years, county workers used Douglas fir logs to help support one of the two spans. The bridge was replaced in 1952. (Courtesy ODOT.)

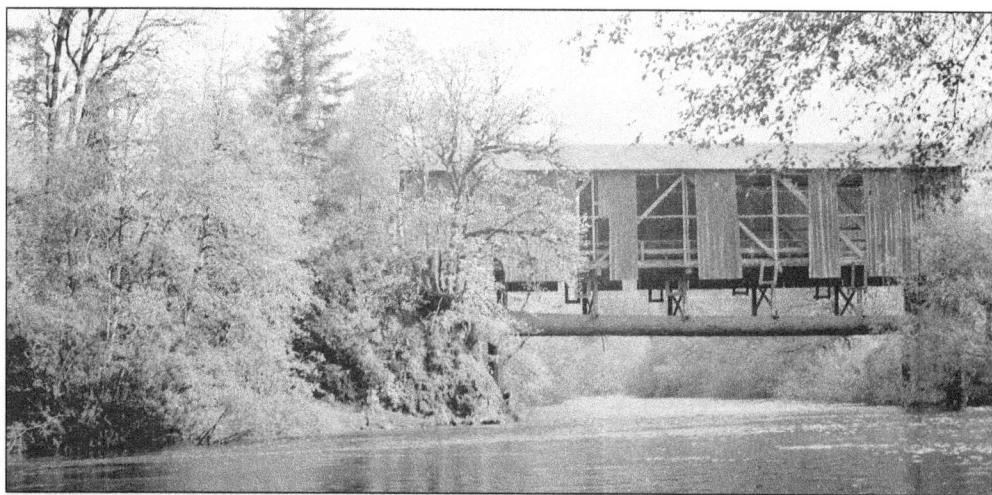

Benefield Bridge spanned the Big Nestucca River about three miles east of Beaver. Tillamook County constructed the wooden bridge, a 100-foot one-span Howe truss, in 1922 for $2,800. The 1942 inspection report read, "Span is badly decayed and is now supported by two 36" Douglas fir logs." The bridge lasted another six years. (Courtesy ODOT.)

Near Blaine, a 60-foot queenpost bridge crossed East Creek. The inspector's 1942 photograph shows the county-built covered span, which cost $1,500 in 1928. His written report stated, "The truss has been supported with log pilings under the floor beams." Vertical clearance for traffic was just 12 feet 2 inches. The bridge was replaced in 1948, when a truck fell through the flooring. (Courtesy ODOT.)

Tillamook County's last covered bridge removed from its landscape was the Frank Cross Bridge. The 60-foot queenpost structure, built in 1915 under private ownership, spanned Three Rivers near Hebo. It was used as a shed or barn during its final years and was lost in 1962. (Courtesy Salem Public Library Historic Photograph Collection.)

Fairdale Bridge passed over the North Yamhill River not far from the famous Flying M Ranch in Yamhill County. A 60-foot Howe truss structure, the bridge was built in 1917 at a cost of just $900. Vertical clearance was 10 feet 6 inches. It was replaced in the 1950s. (Courtesy ODOT.)

This covered span was located about one mile from the Fairdale Bridge. The 84-foot Howe truss was built for Yamhill County in 1917 at a cost of $1,500. Vertical clearance for traffic was just 10 feet 6 inches. The 1942 inspection report said, "No reason why condition of this bridge is so much worse than #11536 [Fairdale Bridge]." (Courtesy ODOT.)

Four

COOS COUNTY

The small community of Bridge took its name from the covered structure in this undated photograph. At this time, the bridge spanned Big Creek. A blacksmith shop, store, post office, and stagecoach stop were a part of the business area. Construction and demolition dates for the bridge have not been found, but the town was relocated when Highway 42 was built in the 1920s. The new road crossed Big Creek within a few yards of where the waters joined the Middle Fork of the Coquille River. Settlers in Coos County began to build covered bridges in the 1870s, when J. D. Bennett and John Fox were hired to construct spans across the Middle Fork. Soon the North Fork and South Fork were spanned with covered bridges. Other streams with covered bridges were Big Creek, Sandy Creek, Rock Creek, and Salmon Creek. The last in the county were built in the 1920s, and only the Sandy Creek Bridge at Remote stands today. (Courtesy Nellie Palmer.)

Spanning the Middle Fork of the Coquille River, this covered bridge was the second at Bridge. The 150-foot Howe truss was built in 1936. Locals often referred to it as the School House Bridge, as it was situated near the school. It lasted until 1969, when it was removed from its piers. (Courtesy ODOT.)

Coos County's last extant covered bridge is the Sandy Creek Bridge at Remote. This 60-foot Howe truss span was built by the firm of A. Guthrie and Company in 1921 for $8,188.63. The highway was subsequently realigned, and the Sandy Creek Bridge has been closed to all but pedestrian traffic since 1949. (Courtesy ODOT.)

A few miles east of the Sandy Creek Bridge, Rock Creek flows into the Middle Fork of the Coquille River. Designed by the state, Rock Creek Bridge was built as a 60-foot Howe truss structure in 1919. The John Hampshire Company constructed the bridge for $6,422.75. It was replaced around 1948. (Courtesy ODOT.)

Several covered Southern Pacific Railroad bridges were built to span the South Fork of the Coquille River for the Smith-Powers Logging Company. Bridge No. 2, pictured here, was a 123-foot Howe truss span constructed in 1922 and covered in 1925. Locals noted that cows often got onto the tracks; a few were killed near Bridge No. 2 when they walked into the side of a moving train. (Courtesy Kildow collection.)

Bridge No. 5 of the Smith-Powers line crossed the South Fork of the Coquille about one mile south of the community of Broadbent. The bridge consisted of two 123-foot Howe trusses. The first span was built in 1921 and the second in 1922; both were covered in 1924. The bridge was destroyed in floodwaters in 1964. (Courtesy Kildow collection.)

About two and one-half miles south of Broadbent, Bridge No. 7 of the Smith-Powers line formed the fourth crossing of the South Fork. Like Bridge No. 5, it was made of two 123-foot Howe trusses. The 40-foot-high bridge was built in 1921 and covered in 1922. It was also lost in the 1964 flood. (Courtesy Kildow collection.)

This covered bridge over Salmon Creek was originally built near the small town of Powers for the Smith-Powers Logging Company in 1923. Steam engines passed through the 130-foot Howe truss bridge for a number of years. Prior to its demolition, it was lowered about four feet, and truck traffic used the bridge until it was closed and eventually destroyed in 1976. The author's 1976 photograph shows its deteriorated condition.

Lone Pine Bridge spanned Middle Creek at the junction of the Coos Bay Wagon Road and the road to Lee Valley near McKinley. It was an 86-foot Howe truss with pile trestle approaches. The exact date of construction is not clear, but locals say J. D. Bennett built a bridge at McKinley in 1907. This 1926 photograph is from the Coos County inspector's file. (Courtesy Coos County Bridge Department.)

Fox Bridge was named in honor of John B. Fox, who settled on the banks of the North Fork of the Coquille River in 1872. Fox paid $10 and an army pistol for the land. Local carpenter J. D. Bennett built this span in 1883. A Smith truss supported the bridge, which lasted until it became a victim of a fire in the 1950s. The remains of the bridge were dismantled in 1954. (Courtesy Salem Public Library Historic Photograph Collection.)

This rustic view shows the Gravelford Bridge alongside Fred Moser's cheese factory and the post office prior to 1917. The covered bridge crossed the North Fork of the Coquille River at Bennett Park, named for bridge builder J. D. Bennett. At some point, the Moser cheese factory caught fire, the blaze spreading to the covered bridge and destroying it. (Courtesy Nellie Palmer.)

After the fire demolished the community of Gravelford, residents relocated to the present site. J. D. Bennett built a covered bridge there in 1917. The 1926 county inspection report describes it as a 126-foot Howe truss with pile trestle approaches. The south approach was 550 feet long and the north approach 70 feet. The date of replacement is unknown. (Courtesy Coos County Bridge Department.)

J. B. Fox reportedly built the North Fork Bridge at Fairview in 1894. It carried a sign reading, "$10 fine for riding or driving faster than a walk over this bridge. J. B. Fox Builder, 1894." Costs of construction totaled $1,800. The bridge was closed to traffic prior to the 1930s. It collapsed a few years later in 1936, and a local family salvaged the timbers to build a barn. (Courtesy Joanne Metcalf.)

The two-span Cooper Covered Bridge, built by George Reidinger in 1890, crossed the North Fork of the Coquille River near Myrtle Point. One of the spans was 90 feet long and the other 130 feet. The bridge was bypassed in 1950, and floodwaters washed it away shortly thereafter. (Courtesy ODOT.)

The first Hoffman Bridge was probably the earliest recognized covered bridge in Coos County. J. B. Fox constructed it in 1879 at the confluence of the Middle and South Forks of the Coquille River to replace a ferry at the site. J. D. Bennett probably built the bridge shown here in 1898, as the county inspection report states it was erected prior to 1902. The 150-foot Howe truss stood about 40 feet above the waterline. (Courtesy Coos County Bridge Department.)

Five

DOUGLAS COUNTY

Not much is known about the first South Dillard Covered Bridge. Built prior to 1900 to span the South Umpqua River about two miles south of Dillard, it was replaced in 1918 with the state-designed two-span Howe truss covered bridge. More than 70 covered bridges once crossed the rivers and creeks of Douglas County. The county's most prolific bridge builder was Floyd C. Frear, who helped construct most of the covered bridges in Douglas County from the 1920s into the 1950s. Frear's inventory of county bridges six days after the October 30, 1950, flood included 34 covered spans. Frear had overseen the construction of 26, including such names as Tyson, Mill Creek, Rochester, Lone Rock, Yokum, Booth, Olalla, and Cavitt Creek. (Courtesy Douglas County Museum.)

Two long covered bridges spanned the South Umpqua River near Dillard. The South Dillard Bridge, located about two miles southeast of town, was a two-span structure built in 1918 by the State of Oregon. It featured Gothic-style windows and a laminated floor. In the 1920s, the individual windows were connected to make a continuous opening for increased visibility. It was replaced with a steel truss span in 1939. (Courtesy ODOT.)

This photograph of the South Dillard Bridge shows work in progress to get the old covered bridge replaced with a new steel truss. (Courtesy ODOT.)

The three-span North Dillard Bridge, about one mile north of Dillard, was built at the same time as the South Dillard span. At 432 feet, it was likely Douglas County's longest covered bridge. This span lasted until 1942 when it was replaced with another three-span wooden truss bridge that was never covered. That bridge was replaced in 1950 with a steel truss. (Courtesy ODOT.)

Sometimes called the Scottsburg Bridge, this structure spanned Mill Creek about four miles west of Scottsburg. Following the standard Howe truss design developed by the Oregon State Highway Commission, contractors E. D. Olds and Sons built the 120-foot bridge in 1925 at a cost of $10,701.33. It lasted just 29 years, being replaced in 1954. (Courtesy ODOT.)

This photograph shows the original Rochester Covered Bridge over Calapooya Creek at the end of its useful life. The exact date of construction is not known, but some records show a covered bridge being built at this location in 1862. This span was replaced with the current structure in 1933. (Courtesy ODOT.)

The original portal opening of the Rochester Bridge bore an "Impaired Clearance" sign. Built in 1933, the bridge includes unusual window shapes on each side. The 80-foot Howe truss spans Calapooya Creek just west of Sutherlin. (Courtesy ODOT.)

Known as the Olivant Covered Bridge, this rustic structure spanned Lookingglass Creek about seven miles west of Roseburg. The 90-foot Smith truss bridge was built in 1905 and replaced in the 1940s. A crude, hand-painted sign advertises a long-forgotten haberdasher, "Duds 4 Men." (Courtesy ODOT.)

Fair Oaks Bridge, a 150-foot Smith truss built in 1910, crossed Calapooya Creek about six miles east of Oakland. Two streams in Oregon are known as Calapooya. Douglas County spells its creek "Calapooya," while Linn County spells its version "Calapooia." (Courtesy ODOT.)

Middle Fork Coquille River Bridge, located near Camas Valley, was designed by the State of Oregon and built in 1922. E. D. Olds served as the prime contractor. Data for the bridge showed an estimated cost of $8,076.30, but the final expenses totaled only $7,373.80. The bridge was a 90-foot Howe truss with two 19-foot approach spans at each end. Middle Fork Bridge was replaced in 1947. (Courtesy ODOT.)

Cavitt Creek Bridge, crossing Little River at the junction with Cavitt Creek, is another of the wooden structures erected by Floyd C. Frear, noted Douglas County bridge builder. The design features odd-shaped portals to accommodate heavy log trucks, and the upper and lower chords use raw logs as members. The bridge continues to handle daily traffic. (Courtesy ODOT.)

Located about two miles east of Glendale, the Barton Park Bridge was transferred from the road department to the parks department when the county restricted its load capacity. Barton Park Bridge, a 135-foot Howe truss spanning Cow Creek, was built for Douglas County by Floyd C. Frear in 1922. It was dismantled in January 1968. (Courtesy ODOT.)

As shown in this 1895 photograph, both the Southern Pacific rail bridge and the Pass Creek Bridge at Drain were covered in the late 19th century. Specific information about these spans is not available, resulting in confusion about the construction date of the current Pass Creek Bridge. Some locals claim it was built in the 1890s or in 1906. Data shows either construction or extensive repairs in 1925. (Courtesy Kildow collection.)

Booth Bridge spanned Elk Creek about five miles northeast of Yoncalla. The 1921 bridge was one of several kingpost truss structures built in the county. Another Frear covered bridge, it measured just 42 feet long. (Courtesy ODOT.)

In 1929, a local named Robert Lancaster built Roaring Camp Bridge for his farm. The 88-foot Howe truss span crossed Elk Creek six miles west of Drain. In its final years of service, the private bridge served two families as well as the tourists who stopped to view the sagging structure. It was demolished in the summer of 1995. (Courtesy ODOT.)

Located 12 miles south of Scottsburg in western Douglas County, the McDonald Bridge spanned Lake Creek at the Loon Lake inlet. The unusual portal openings were designed to handle log trucks. Douglas County bridge builder Floyd C. Frear oversaw construction of the 60-foot Howe truss in 1932. The bridge was replaced in 1970. (Courtesy ODOT.)

Celebrants at the Cavitt Creek Bridge head toward an outing near Glide, east of Roseburg. The probable date of construction is the 1880s, but the replacement date is unknown. Unidentified participants include the local Strader and Baker families. (Courtesy Douglas County Museum.)

Seen here in 1905, the old covered bridge at Glendale spanned Cow Creek. The lumber flume parallel with Cow Creek was built for the Lystal and Lawson Mill or for the Glendale Lumber Company. (Courtesy Douglas County Museum.)

Yokum Bridge was originally a one-span 105-foot Howe truss bridge across Cow Creek. Completed in 1922, it included 257 feet of timber approach spans. An additional 75-foot covered span was constructed to complement the original span in 1927. The builder of both covered spans was Floyd C. Frear. Yokum Bridge was replaced in 1958. (Courtesy ODOT.)

54

The bridge crew and family members pose at the Tiller Bridge in 1889. This bridge spanned the South Umpqua River near the small Tiller community, lasting only until 1891, when floodwaters washed it downstream. This is the only known photograph of the bridge. (Courtesy Douglas County Museum.)

Worthington Bridge was under construction when this photograph was taken around 1910. The one-span Smith truss structure passed over the South Umpqua River near Canyonville. Worthington Bridge was abandoned in the 1950s and soon un-housed. Adpheus Fields built this wooden span. (Courtesy Douglas County Museum.)

In 1918, Hogan Bridge was built to span Calapooya Creek about four miles west of Sutherlin in Douglas County. Four exterior buttresses on each side stabilized it. This technique was unique in Douglas and Jackson Counties. After the bridge's replacement in 1954, county employees burned the old structure. (Courtesy Kildow collection.)

A horse-drawn hay wagon driven by Arthur Mack passes through the Elkton Covered Bridge over Elk Creek in the early 1900s. The Smith truss bridge was built in 1909 and replaced in 1931. This photograph is suggestive of a slower-paced lifestyle. (Courtesy Douglas County Museum.)

The old Quines Creek Covered Bridge, a Smith truss built in 1913, spanned Cow Creek near Azalea. The vital wooden truss members deteriorated over the years. Eventually, in 1958, the 100-foot bridge was replaced. At that time, it was likely Oregon's last covered span of Smith truss construction. (Courtesy Salem Public Library Historic Photograph Collection.)

Lone Rock Covered Bridge crossed the wild waters of the North Umpqua River near the town of Glide. One of many state-designed covered spans built by counties during and following World War I, it was erected in 1922 as a substitute for a river ferry. Douglas County engineer Elmer Metzer supervised construction of the three-span Howe truss. Costs to build the bridge totaled $15,400. It was replaced in 1959. (Courtesy Salem Public Library Historic Photograph Collection.)

Little is known about Douglas County's Fall Creek Bridge, but this photograph deserves publication. The bridge actually spanned Little River and was constructed during the 1880s, but the length and truss type are uncertain. Here participants are on their way to Fourth of July festivities around 1900. (Courtesy Douglas County Museum.)

Located in a rural setting in Douglas County, Stephens Covered Bridge spanned Calapooya Creek about 12 miles west of Sutherlin. Square windows graced each side of the bridge. The old 120-foot Smith truss structure was built in 1903 and lasted into the 1950s. (Courtesy ODOT.)

Fate Covered Bridge was a 100-foot structure built in 1920 to cross the South Umpqua River about a half-mile south of Milo. Although a private bridge, it was used as a detour during the construction of the main route in 1932. The span lasted until its replacement in 1960. (Courtesy ODOT.)

The old Fate Bridge was either rebuilt or rehoused for use by the Seventh Day Adventist Academy. This 1956 photograph shows the Milo Academy Bridge (Fate Bridge) with exterior buttresses to stabilize it against vibration and wind forces. The bridge was replaced with a steel girder span in 1960. (Courtesy Leroy G. Gates and Joseph Conwill.)

The Oregon and California Railroad constructed a number of covered bridges along its route in western Oregon. This one, spanning the West Fork of Cow Creek, was built in 1882 and replaced in 1906. (Courtesy Douglas County Museum.)

When the Fate Bridge was replaced with a steel girder span, locals decided to add sides and a roof to the structure for sentimental reasons. Now known as the Milo Academy Bridge, it continues to carry people across the South Umpqua River. (Courtesy ODOT.)

Oregon's remaining kingpost truss is the Neal Lane Bridge in the small town of Myrtle Creek. The 42-foot bridge was built in 1929. (Courtesy ODOT.)

In 1925, Douglas County constructed a covered bridge over Coffee Creek, 20 miles east of Canyonville, for $4,065.25. The 36-foot kingpost structure with 179 feet of approach spans rested on concrete piers. Inspection reports show an alternative spelling of "Coffey." The bridge was replaced in 1942. (Courtesy ODOT.)

Turpin Bridge spanned Elk Creek a short distance from Yoncalla. Floyd C. Frear supervised the construction of the little 42-foot kingpost in 1921. The bridge survived until its replacement in April 1950. (Courtesy Kildow collection.)

Six

JACKSON COUNTY

In this 1975 photograph, the 58-foot queenpost Antelope Creek Bridge has been bypassed from traffic. Built by Lyle and Wes Hartman in 1922, it survived in the rural Jackson County countryside until being moved to Eagle Point in 1987. It was then rebuilt as a pedestrian bridge over Butte Creek. The Howe truss so widely used throughout the west was virtually unknown in Jackson County. Bridge builders used the queenpost truss or a modified queenpost for the county's bridge support system. Typically, these covered spans were shorter in length. They used exterior flying buttresses for stabilization and shorter protective portal weatherboarding. More than 35 covered bridges were discovered in Jackson County. Today only three survive, with one to be rebuilt soon at Wimer.

Rock Point Covered Bridge, crossing the Rogue River near Gold Hill, was a two-span structure built in 1880. Although it appeared neglected by maintenance crews, the old bridge survived until 1922, when it was replaced with a concrete arch bridge. (Courtesy ODOT.)

Eagle Point Bridge spanned Little Butte Creek near the town of Eagle Point on Medford–Crater Lake Road. Old county files show that the 60-foot queenpost structure was built in 1880–1881. It was replaced by a 60-foot steel deck truss bridge in 1921. (Courtesy ODOT.)

The Antelope Creek Covered Bridge was built near the town of Eagle Point on the old Medford–Crater Lake Road in 1901–1902. It passed over Antelope Creek about one mile from the Eagle Point Bridge, which crossed Little Butte Creek. This bridge gave way to a reinforced concrete span in August 1921. (Courtesy ODOT.)

Crossing Evans Creek, Minthorn Bridge typified the Jackson County construction standards with a shingle roof, wooden decking, rounded portal openings, and exterior buttress stabilizers. This bridge, supported by a 57-foot queenpost truss, was built in 1927 by Lyle and Wes Hartman. The 1964 Christmas Day flood severely damaged the structure, and it was removed shortly thereafter. (Courtesy ODOT.)

This little queenpost bridge, known as the Yankee Creek Covered Bridge, was built in 1922 by Lyle and Wes Hartman. The 44-foot span was located about 12 miles northeast of Medford on Yankee Creek Road, about one mile from the Antelope Creek Bridge. After the Yankee Creek structure was replaced in 1974, county workers burned the timbers, leaving only smoldering embers for the protesters who favored saving the bridge. (Courtesy ODOT.)

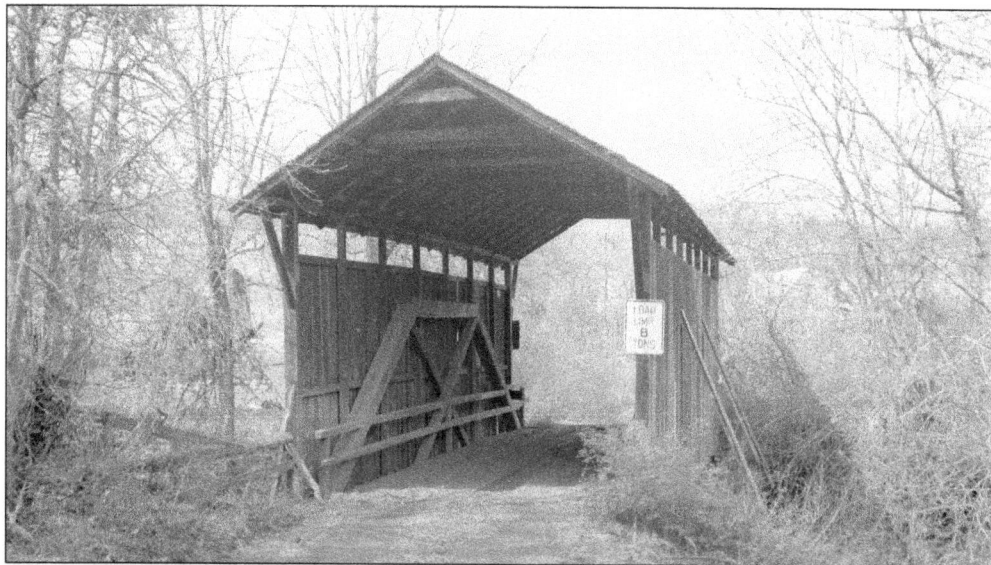

Lost Creek Bridge spans Lost Creek east of Medford. Locals still argue over the construction date, with some claiming 1881 and others saying 1919. For many years, the 39-foot bridge crossed Lost Creek without portal boards on both ends. In the early 1990s, however, workers restored the queenpost span with the installation of new portal boards. Exterior buttresses stabilize the structure. At the time of its restoration, the bridge was bypassed with a nearby concrete span. (Courtesy ODOT.)

On July 6, 2003, the Wimer Covered Bridge sadly collapsed, injuring three people. The collapse also hurt the pride of the local community, as it had been home to a covered bridge since 1892. The Wimer Bridge pictured here was the second, built in 1927 by Lyle and Wes Hartman. The 85-foot queenpost truss featured exterior stabilizing buttresses. (Courtesy ODOT.)

Jason Hartman built the McKee Bridge on land donated by Adelbert "Deb" McKee in 1917. The bridge was used from 1917 to 1956, originally serving the needs of the Blue Ledge Copper Mine near the California border. Usually, two stagecoaches and many wagons of ore crossed the wooden covered bridge each day. The 122-foot Howe truss structure, sitting on concrete piers, is now bypassed and permits only pedestrian traffic. (Courtesy ODOT.)

This bridge originally served traffic on Crater Lake Highway about nine miles northeast of Medford. Built in 1901–1902, it was moved to Riley Road in 1921 and shortened several feet to span Antelope Creek. The old Riley Road Covered Bridge was finally replaced in 1959. (Courtesy Kildow collection.)

Lyle and Wes Hartman constructed Peyton Bridge with exterior buttresses, as per the old Jackson County style, in 1919. The span, also known as Laurelhurst Bridge, crossed Rogue River eight miles southwest of Prospect. The 120-foot bridge was removed in 1961. (Courtesy Kildow collection.)

Seven

LANE COUNTY

This 1907 photograph shows Lord "Nels" Roney's crew on the 190-foot Lowell Bridge truss. This bridge lasted 37 years, slightly longer than the other 100 spans that Roney's crew built during his tenure. The Lowell Bridge spanned the Middle Fork of the Willamette River until being replaced with the current covered bridge. Covered bridge construction began in earnest in the 1870s when contractors A. S. Miller and Sons established an office in Eugene. Many of the firm's bridges were washed away in the gigantic flood of 1881. Beginning in 1881 and continuing for 20 years, Roney competed with Miller for bridge construction. In the 1920s, the county began using its own crews to build bridges rather than bidding the jobs out. During the 1920s and 1930s, the county included more than 120 roofed spans. Lane County continued to build covered bridges well into the 1940s and even the 1950s. County workers not only constructed most of the existing covered bridges, but also built the uncovered ones to replace the old housed bridges. (Courtesy Lane County Historical Museum.)

Scenery around the Lowell Bridge has changed drastically since this photograph was taken in the late 1940s. The Middle Fork of the Willamette River was a free-flowing stream until the dam and reservoir were built. The bridge was constructed in 1945 but not covered until county workers returned from World War II. A 165-foot Howe truss, the Lowell Bridge was extensively rehabilitated in 2006 into an interpretative center. (Courtesy Kildow collection.)

Here the two-span Hendricks Covered Bridge is constructed over the McKenzie River in 1907. One span was 240 feet long and the other 180 feet. W. W. Inman built the bridge, which was replaced in 1925. (Courtesy Lane County Historical Museum.)

Lane County built this Long Tom River bridge under the management of county bridge supervisor G. W. Breeding in 1921. The 60-foot Howe truss span was sometimes called the Second Crossing Bridge. Construction costs totaled $4,597.32. Vertical clearance was 15 feet, necessitating the enlargement of the portal openings in the 1940s. The bridge was replaced in 1950. (Courtesy ODOT.)

Portage Bridge was one of several covered bridges to span the North Fork of the Siuslaw River, not far from Mapleton. In 1930, it was constructed by the county under the supervision of A. C. Striker. Costs were limited to $2,330.78 by using county employees and local timber. The 60-foot Howe truss span was replaced in the mid-1960s. (Courtesy ODOT.)

Folklore relates a tale of a family living in this Indian Creek Covered Bridge for several weeks during a rainy season in the 1920s. The dirt road became impassable as the dirt turned into deep mud, and the horses could not pull the family's wagon any farther. A. N. Striker built the bridge in 1903. The 70-foot Howe truss lasted until 1929, when it gave way to a concrete bridge. This 1929 photograph shows the original just prior to replacement. (Courtesy ODOT.)

Shown here is the second Mary White Covered Bridge to span the Coast Fork of the Willamette River. It was erected in 1929 to replace the prior covered span, which had been built in 1905. Lane County bridge supervisor A. C. Striker, son of A. N. Striker, oversaw construction. With local materials and county workers, costs totaled $8,841.76. The 90-foot Howe truss was replaced in 1965, following the disastrous flood of the previous year. (Courtesy ODOT.)

Lane Co at Saginaw. 18 Mi. S. of Eugene. Coast Fk. Willamette. 140' Tr. Built 1884

The first Saginaw Covered Bridge crossed the Coast Fork of the Willamette River. Well-known bridge builder Nels Roney constructed the old Howe truss structure in 1884. When floodwaters damaged the timbers in 1942, the bridge was removed in December of that year. (Courtesy ODOT.)

The second Saginaw Covered Bridge was a 165-foot Howe truss designed by the Oregon Department of Transportation and built in 1943. Labor and materials totaled $19,055. This bridge was replaced with a concrete span in 1965. (Courtesy ODOT.)

This Long Tom River covered bridge, known as the Sailor-Knight Bridge, is located on the Eugene-Swisshome Highway. The 64-foot Howe truss span was built by Lane County in 1925. This maintenance work was recorded in 1940: "Paint housing and handrail, re-stain roof green, cinch bolt top chord, take up truss rods and tighten bolts." In 1950, more work was detailed: "Replace deck and all stringers, place two additional stringers in truss, replace decayed piling in piers on each end." The bridge was replaced in 1962. (Courtesy ODOT.)

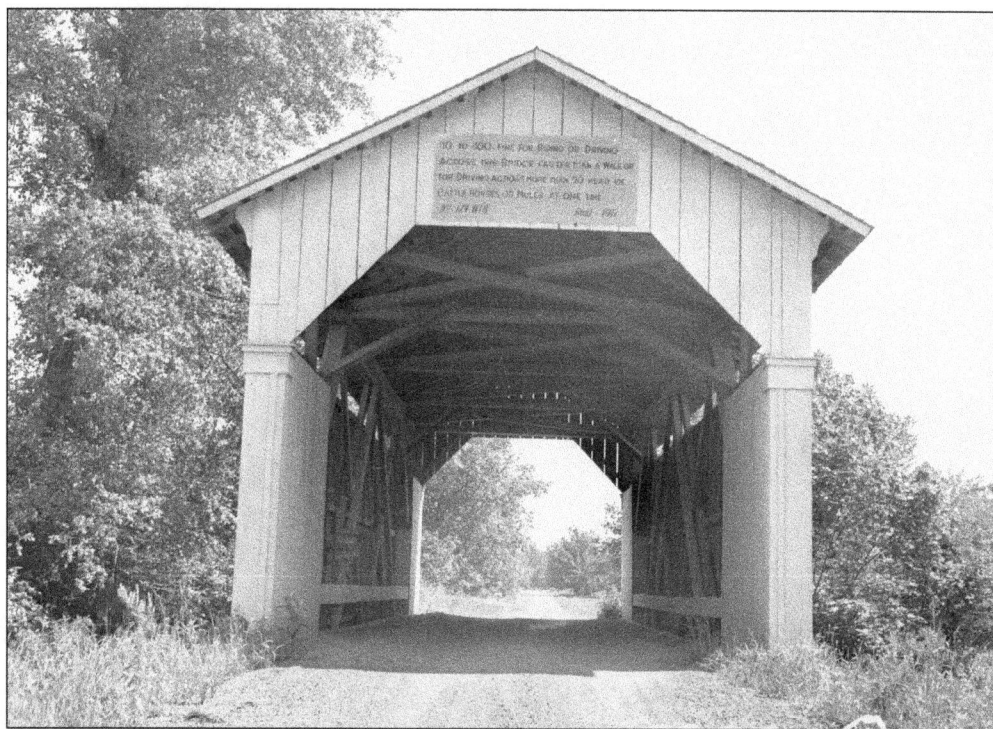

This bridge near Firgrove was a 60-foot Howe truss span over backwater at Gallagher Slough. In 1917, W. O. Heckart built it at a cost of $1,767.55. The 1943 inspection report noted the stream choked by brush and the bridge decking worn and rough. The sign posted on the bridge stated, "$10 to $100 fine for riding or driving across this bridge faster than a walk or for driving across more than 20 head of cattle, horses, or mules at one time. Built 1917." A culvert eventually replaced the bridge. (Courtesy ODOT.)

Walton Bridge spanned Gallagher Slough near Firgrove, north of Eugene. At least four covered bridges crossed backwaters of the Willamette River in this area of Lane County. W. W. Inman constructed the 60-foot Howe truss structure in 1916 at a cost of $1,180. Walton Bridge gave way to a concrete culvert. (Courtesy ODOT.)

Spanning the slough on Beacon Drive north of Eugene, River Loop Bridge was a 50-foot Howe truss built in 1932 by Lane County. The Beacon Drive Bridge can be seen in the background, through this structure. The 1943 inspection report noted worn and unsurfaced decking. The stringers were at about 80 percent, as decay was found in the timbers. The bridge was replaced with a concrete culvert in the 1950s. (Courtesy ODOT.)

The first Brumbaugh Bridge, supported by a 92-foot Howe truss, was built in 1925 for just $3,800. Each panel of the six-panel bridge ran 15 feet 4 inches. Both the top and bottom chords measured 12 by 12 inches. Roof rafters were 2 by 4 inches on 24-inch centers. The housing consisted of 1-by-12-inch boards with 1-by-4-inch battens. Overhead clearance was 14 feet 8 inches. This bridge was replaced with a covered span in 1948. (Courtesy ODOT.)

This photograph, taken by the author in 1976, shows the second Brumbaugh Covered Bridge in its final years of service. The county constructed it in 1948 for $13,931. Wooden pilings supported the bridge, and horizontal wooden boards attached to the piers kept debris from accumulating underneath. The structure used the standard 90-foot Howe truss and state-designed portals. Deteriorating timbers caused the county to replace the bridge in 1979. Pieces of the Brumbaugh Covered Bridge were used to build the centennial covered pedestrian bridge in downtown Cottage Grove.

The Lower Brice Creek Bridge spanned Brice Creek near Culp Creek, south of Cottage Grove. According to state records, the six-panel, 90-foot Howe truss was constructed by Lane County in 1927. In 1945, the inspector rated the deck, stringers, and abutments at 65 percent. The bridge was replaced in the early 1960s. (Courtesy ODOT.)

Located about one mile from the Lower Brice Creek Bridge, the Upper Brice Creek Bridge was built in 1935 by Lane County under the management of bridge superintendent A. C. Striker. The 90-foot Howe truss bridge was supported by wooden log crib piers. Roof rafters were 2-by-4-inch boards on 26-inch centers. The housing consisted of 1-by-12-inch boards with 1-by-4-inch battens. The 1945 inspection rated the bridge at 65 percent, and it was replaced in the early 1960s. (Courtesy ODOT.)

This covered bridge, built in 1904 at a cost of $2,950, spanned the Row River south of Cottage Grove and east of Culp Creek. The 93-foot-6-inch housed truss structure had six panels at 15 feet 7 inches each. The bridge rested on 12-by-12-inch log cribs. Overhead clearance was 14 feet. The top and bottom chords consisted of timbers measuring 12 by 12 inches. Rafters were 2-by-4-inch boards on 26-inch centers. The housing was made up of 1-by-12-inch boards with 1-by-4-inch battens. The 1945 inspection deemed the bridge 80 percent good. It was replaced in the 1950s. (Courtesy ODOT.)

For this white bridge, Lane County kept the name Red Bridge, the color of the previous structure. The author interviewed bridge supervisor Miller Sorensen, who recalled that his crew camped out for three months in 1928 building this covered span. A local farmer killed hogs and a steer to help feed the hungry bridge crew. In 1960, the county constructed a concrete span in its place. (Courtesy ODOT.)

Bridge supervisor Miller Sorensen remembered the Mapleton Bridge as his favorite covered bridge. He oversaw the hiring of numerous Civilian Conservation Corps "boys" during the construction in 1934. Mapleton Bridge was a two-span, 210-foot Howe truss with a lift span for river traffic. That lift was never opened. The bridge was replaced with a concrete structure in 1970. (Courtesy Salem Public Library Historic Photograph Collection.)

This 1934 photograph shows the bridge crew supervised by Miller Sorensen at Mapleton. Most of the workers were members of the Civilian Conservation Corps. (Courtesy ODOT.)

In 1930, Lane County workers built the Champion Creek Bridge, a 60-foot Howe truss covered span. Bridge supervisor A. C. Striker oversaw construction. It spanned Champion Creek several miles southeast of Disston near Lund Park. The 1945 inspection showed the decks and stringers rated at 50 percent, and the bridge was replaced in the 1950s. (Courtesy ODOT.)

A 75-foot Howe truss structure, Sharps Creek Bridge was constructed over several weeks in 1922, during which county employees camped out at the site. Overhead clearance was limited to just 13 feet 11 inches. In 1945, the inspector noted the weakened bridge to be only at 40 percent. The old structure was replaced within a few short years. (Courtesy ODOT.)

Ole Haldorson recalled that the Lane County bridge crew, of which he was part, built the Belknap Bridge during the winter months in 1939. On most days, workers wore calked boots for traction, as the timbers were iced over. Costs of construction totaled $4,100. During the 1964 flood, a large tree with a giant rootball speared the bridge housing. The raging water of the McKenzie River pushed the rootball under the bridge, twisting the structure from its pilings. A new covered span was completed in 1965. (Courtesy ODOT.)

Hemlock Bridge crossed the North Fork of the Willamette River just a short distance downstream from the Office Bridge at Westfir. When the Office Bridge washed out in the 1942 flood, the local mill used the Hemlock Bridge to truck logs and finished timber across the river. The 100-foot span cost $3,900 to build. Lane County replaced the old wooden bridge with concrete in the 1950s. (Courtesy ODOT.)

Lane County built the Salt Creek Bridge in 1927. The six-panel, 90-foot Howe truss structure spanned Salt Creek not far from Oakridge, near the Willamette Pass. Although inspection reports in the 1940s showed the bridge in good condition, the county replaced the old structure in 1955. (Courtesy ODOT.)

Meadows Bridge spanned the North Fork of the Siuslaw River near Minerva in western Lane County. County workers built the 105-foot Howe truss bridge in 1922. The portal opening height was just 13 feet 10 inches. Not much vehicular traffic used the bridge due to its isolated location. Costs of maintenance necessitated replacement in 1979. (Courtesy ODOT.)

This 1938 photograph shows the new Pengra Bridge alongside the old bridge trusses. The old span was a 192-foot covered bridge built in 1904. The new one is a 120-foot Howe truss that uses single logs for both the upper and lower chords. Ole Haldorson, a member of the bridge crew, said that it took about a day and a half to hand-shape each of the large trees into chords for the truss. (Courtesy ODOT.)

In this 1945 photograph, Dorena Bridge inhabits a rural setting near the dam at Dorena Lake. Lane County built the 105-foot Howe truss structure in 1930. A year before the bridge was destroyed, its condition was rated at 70 percent. A new Dorena Bridge was built at the upper end of the lake in 1949. (Courtesy ODOT.)

This bridge, a 75-foot Howe truss span built in 1926, crossed Hills Creek a short distance from Kitson Springs in eastern Lane County. In 1945, the inspector noted deficiencies and rated the overall condition at 50 percent. The bridge was replaced prior to 1950. (Courtesy ODOT.)

Built in 1944, the 180-foot Office Bridge replaced an earlier covered bridge that washed out in 1942. The inclusion of a covered pedestrian walkway was rare in Oregon. Lane County took ownership of the bridge when the timber company went bankrupt. It was extensively rehabilitated in 1993. (Courtesy ODOT.)

Lane County employees built the McLeod Creek Bridge in 1928 at a cost of just $1,116.01. The 45-foot queenpost was located in western Lane County near Bickersville. The county replaced the little wooden structure with a log-stringer bridge in 1949. (Courtesy ODOT.)

In 1930, Lane County workers constructed the Horse Creek Bridge at a cost of $2,452.44, replacing a 103-foot covered bridge built by A. N. Striker in 1904. The bridge pictured here was closed to traffic in the 1960s and left standing. Moved to Douglas County, it was rebuilt in Myrtle Creek in 1993. (Courtesy ODOT.)

The Little River Bridge at Blackbutte was another that spanned the Coast Fork of the Willamette River in Lane County. The state-designed bridge was built by Lane County in 1932 at a cost of $3,900. The 75-foot Howe truss bridge, situated about one mile north of Blackbutte, lasted until its replacement in 1950. The Little River Bridge replaced an earlier covered bridge that had been built here in 1905. (Courtesy ODOT.)

A 75-foot Howe truss structure, the Rouse Bridge was built in 1937 at a cost of $4,300. The top chords were 12-by-14-inch timbers, and the bottom chords were 14-by-14-inch timbers. The Rouse Bridge was a victim of the infamous 1964 flood. Raging waters dropped one end into the Coast Fork of the Willamette River, resulting in the bridge's replacement in 1965. (Courtesy ODOT.)

Most photographs of the Thorne Covered Bridge show splintered portal boards on both ends—a result of loaded logging trucks. Built by Lane County in 1925 at a cost of $4,567.62, the roofed bridge crossed the Coast Fork of the Willamette River near Cottage Grove. The 120-foot Howe truss structure consisted of eight panels at 15 feet each. The bridge was replaced in the late 1950s. (Courtesy ODOT.)

In 1921, George W. Breeding and his crew constructed the 75-foot Howe truss Parvin Bridge over Lost Creek near Dexter. Construction costs reached only $3,617.82, including the approach spans. This bridge replaced a prior covered bridge that had been built in 1890. In 1917, the inspector mused, "An old bridge. Chords badly worm eaten. Wood is little better than powder from worm action." (Courtesy ODOT.)

Lane County built the Hills Creek Bridge over Hills Creek near Jasper in 1940. The county expended only $2,700 in construction costs due to the use of county workers. This 60-foot Howe truss structure was replaced prior to 1960. Note the log flume to the right of the bridge. (Courtesy ODOT.)

Marcola Bridge spanned the Mohawk River at the edge of the small community of Marcola. Lane County constructed the covered span in 1936 under the supervision of bridge superintendent A. C. Striker. The 75-foot Howe truss cost the county just $3,187.69. Marcola Bridge gave way to a concrete structure in 1966. (Courtesy ODOT.)

Lane County workers built the Smith Cut Bridge over the North Fork of the Siuslaw River in 1930. It was a five-panel, 75-foot Howe truss bridge with cedar abutments. A log truck damaged the bridge, and the covered span was replaced with a log bridge in the mid-1950s. (Courtesy ODOT.)

The rustic little Noti Creek Bridge crossed Noti Creek in a rural countryside environment. Lane County constructed the 42-foot bridge in 1927 at a low cost of $790. The wooden deck had a 3-by-12-inch running plank for traffic. Little maintenance was performed on this bridge, as the 1944 inspection report recommended immediate replacement. At that time, the abutments, deck, stringers, and truss were rated at just 15 percent. The inspector noted, "This one couldn't function as a truss." (Courtesy ODOT.)

Steinhauer Bridge, spanning the West Fork of Deadwood Creek in western Lane County, was a 45-foot Howe truss structure built in 1920 for $750. Overhead clearance was just 12 feet 7 inches. The inspection in 1943 indicated serious problems and recommended replacement: "Structure too much patched. Traffic very light. Structure should be replaced. Does not act as truss." The old bridge was replaced in 1952. (Courtesy ODOT.)

Wolf Creek Bridge crossed the creek just a few feet from its confluence with the Siuslaw River and about six miles south of Austa. The 60-foot Howe truss consisted of four panels at 15 feet each and a roof of cedar shingles. A county crew built the bridge in 1926 for $1,700. Both the top and bottom chords were timbers measuring 12 by 12 inches. The siding boards measured 1 by 12 inches. This bridge was replaced in the 1950s. (Courtesy ODOT.)

Eight

LINCOLN COUNTY

Fuller Bridge was one of three covered bridges constructed by the firm of Monson Trierweiler and Company to span the Siletz River in Lincoln County. This bridge passed over the river about three-quarters of a mile north of Siletz. Construction was completed on December 1, 1922, at a cost totaling $17,149.05. The 190-foot Howe truss bridge lasted just 24 years and was replaced in 1946. The misty, wet air of coastal Lincoln County usually reduced the lifespan of covered bridges. The county adopted a unique pattern of construction for its covered bridges that included shingled roofs, rounded portals, flared sides, board-batten siding, crosswise plank flooring, and a coat of red paint. More than 45 covered bridge sites dotted the landscape in the 1920s and 1930s. These bridges spanned streams named the Yachats River, Five Rivers, Yaquina River, Siletz River, Alsea River, Schooner Creek, and Drift Creek. The county usually constructed the covered bridges, but the best-known local builder was Otis Hamar, who oversaw the completion of the Sam Creek, Chitwood, and North Fork Yachats Bridges. (Courtesy Salem Public Library Historic Photograph Collection.)

Lincoln County includes two separate Drift Creeks. The bridge pictured here (No. 11491), spanning the southern Drift Creek near Waldport, was constructed by the county in 1923 at a cost of $3,000. It remained uncovered for several years. After workers completed the housing, the vertical clearance was just 12 feet. The 84-foot Howe truss structure lasted only into the 1950s. (Courtesy ODOT.)

This Southern Drift Creek bridge (No. 11492), identical to No. 11491, was built about one mile away. The 84-foot Howe truss cost the county $3,000. This 1940s inspector's photograph shows his Woody wagon at the bridge site. (Courtesy ODOT.)

Lincoln County built the Slick Rock Creek Bridge in 1930. Sometimes known as Rose Lodge Bridge, it spanned Slick Rock Creek about two miles from the small community of Rose Lodge. The 42-foot queenpost structure lasted until its replacement in 1963. (Courtesy ODOT.)

Supported by a 62-foot Howe truss, this old covered bridge over Schooner Creek cost the county just $1,200 to construct in 1914. Not much vehicular traffic passed through the bridge due to its rural location. However, in 1963, a county road grader fell through the decking, and the bridge was replaced shortly thereafter. (Courtesy ODOT.)

The original site for the Northern Drift Creek Bridge was about one mile from the Pacific Ocean near Taft. This 1960 photograph shows the old bridge and the large spruce tree that would be blown down during the Columbus Day storm in 1962. The bridge survived but was closed to traffic within a few years. In 1997, the Drift Creek Bridge was dismantled and moved to Bear Creek, where it was rebuilt on private property. It is open to the public. (Courtesy Salem Public Library Historic Photograph Collection.)

About seven miles up Yachats River Road, this covered bridge spanned the Yachats River. The county expended just $800 for the completed 57-foot Howe truss bridge in 1932. This Yachats River bridge was replaced with an 80-foot concrete span in 1955. (Courtesy ODOT.)

Another of the Yachats River covered bridges, this 40-foot queenpost truss was located about nine and one half miles east of Yachats. Lincoln County paid $1,500 for the bridge in 1928. It gave way to a concrete span in 1957. (Courtesy ODOT.)

Still farther up Yachats River Road was the covered bridge pictured here, a 48-foot Howe truss built in 1927 and spanning the river at milepost 9.7. Costs to construct this little covered span were just $2,000. The bridge lasted until 1956, when it was replaced. (Courtesy ODOT.)

Like Yachats River, Five Rivers hosted several covered bridges. This 54-foot Howe truss was constructed over Five Rivers in 1927 at a sum of $3,500. The bridge contained many standard Lincoln County features, including a shingled roof, rounded portal openings, wooden deck flooring, slanted sides, and barn-red paint on the housing. It was later replaced with a concrete bridge. (Courtesy ODOT.)

Fisher School Bridge over Five Rivers was built either in 1919 or 1927, depending upon which records one reviews. The 72-foot Howe truss bridge, whose construction costs totaled $1,800, was located about nine miles from Highway 34. It was bypassed when a new concrete span was built. In 2005, the bridge was dismantled and rebuilt about 50 feet downstream from its original site. The author's 1975 photograph shows the structure in poor condition.

For many years, travelers had to cross the Tidewater Bridge to get to the Five Rivers area. The 130-foot Howe truss covered span was built in 1934 at a cost of $5,000. Many users complained that they felt like they were driving through a tunnel when crossing. Tidewater Bridge was replaced in 1961. (Courtesy ODOT.)

Little Lobster Creek Bridge displayed most of the usual Lincoln County features such as wooden piers, a shingled roof, oval portals, and a wooden deck floor system. A 45-foot queenpost, the bridge was built in 1933 for just $580. The oddity involves its location. This bridge actually spanned Little Lobster Creek in Benton County, not Lincoln County. An interagency agreement between the counties provided the necessary maintenance for the bridge. It was replaced in 1957. (Courtesy ODOT.)

In 1922, Otis Hamar supervised construction of the Sam Creek Bridge across the Siletz River about five miles from Siletz. Tall concrete piers—not the wooden pilings prevalent in Lincoln County covered bridges—supported this 100-foot Howe truss structure. Hamar's bid to construct the bridge was just $4,000. It served the needs of the area until being bypassed in 1961. It was finally dismantled in 1981. (Courtesy ODOT.)

Mill Creek Bridge was a 36-foot queenpost truss bridge built in 1929. The little span cost just $1,600 to construct. Vertical clearance was 12 feet. In some photographs, the portal boards show damage from high loads. This roofed bridge was replaced in 1961. (Courtesy ODOT.)

The Yaquina River provided the stream for the Thornton Bridge, which was constructed by Lincoln County in 1924 at a cost of $3,200. The 84-foot Howe truss was located about one mile west of the small community of Chitwood. It was replaced in 1971. (Courtesy ODOT.)

Pioneer Bridge spanned the Yaquina River near the post office of the small community of Pioneer. The 72-foot Howe truss wooden bridge was built in 1924 and replaced in 1955. (Courtesy ODOT.)

The covered bridge at Elk City crossed the Yaquina River. Lincoln County paid $3,200 for construction of the 100-foot Howe truss span in 1922. Over time, the wooden pilings that supported the bridge rotted. This photograph, taken by the author in 1977, shows the bridge just four years prior to destruction. It was destroyed during rehabilitation in 1981 when strong winds blew the bridge from the cranes lifting it for repair.

Lincoln County completed the construction of the Deer Creek Bridge in 1921 at a cost of $1,400. The 36-foot queenpost structure spanned Deer Creek in its remote location until being replaced in 1960. (Courtesy ODOT.)

In 1934, Feagles Bridge was built over Big Elk Creek not far from Elk City on the Feagles–Spout Creek Road. The 66-foot Howe truss structure cost $1,250 to build. It exhibited rounded portals and flared sides, along with a shingle roof. It was replaced in the 1960s. (Courtesy ODOT.)

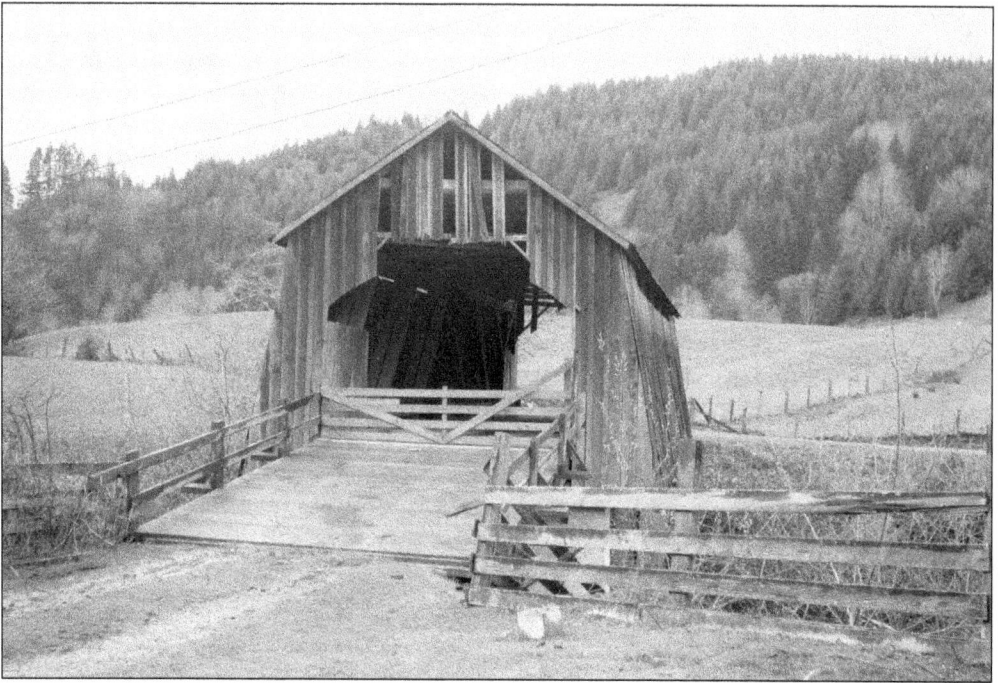

Not many covered bridges revert from public use to private use like the Salado Bridge. In its final years of service, it was used as a barn. The bridge was built in 1921 to span Big Elk Creek. Locals sometimes referred to the 72-foot Howe truss structure as Hill Top Bridge. The bridge, which cost $5,000 to complete, finally collapsed in 1967. (Courtesy ODOT.)

This 1936 photograph displays the 100-foot Howe truss bridge that crossed Schooner Creek on the Coast Highway near Taft. The Federal Bureau of Public Roads oversaw the design and construction of this roofed span in 1924. Construction expenditures totaled $14,824.99, and an exterior walkway was added several years after completion. The bridge was replaced after World War II. (Courtesy Salem Public Library Historic Photograph Collection.)

Nine

LINN COUNTY

The covered bridge at Stayton was part of a three-span bridge across the North Santiam River, the dividing line between Marion and Linn Counties. This 1946 photograph reveals the dilapidated condition of the old wooden span, which was built in 1912 and measured 83 feet long. The other two spans were steel truss structures. The wooden span was replaced in 1951. Settlers began arriving in the Linn County area in the 1840s, and soon towns began to develop. By the 1850s, crude wooden bridges passed over streams along trails and dirt roads. As these old bridges deteriorated or washed away, they were replaced with covered bridges. A. S. Miller and others constructed bridges over the North and South Santiam Rivers, Thomas Creek, Crabtree Creek, and Calapooia River. More than 80 covered bridge sites have been identified within the county. The Smith truss supported early bridges, but most builders used the Howe truss in later years. Today there are only eight covered bridges left in the county. (Courtesy Salem Public Library Historic Photograph Collection.)

A very long and dark bridge to cross, Sanderson Bridge was a three-span structure measuring 609 feet in length (each of the spans was 203 feet). It crossed the South Santiam River about a half-mile from Crabtree. The old bridge was severely damaged in the 1921 flood. Emergency repairs reopened the bridge, but it was replaced in 1934. (Courtesy ODOT.)

Foster Bridge was a two-span Howe truss structure built about a half-mile from Foster. One truss was 135 feet in length, and the other was 105 feet. Construction was completed in 1940 at a total cost of about $13,000. When the dam was built in 1966, this bridge was burned. It had a short life of just 26 years. (Courtesy ODOT.)

This 1960 photograph shows both the covered road bridge and the covered rail bridge spanning Thomas Creek at Gilkey. The road bridge, built in 1939, is a 120-foot Howe truss structure that was extensively rehabilitated in 1998. The rail span, No. 700.99, was a 125-foot Howe truss bridge for the Southern Pacific Railroad. It was removed in 1962. (Courtesy Salem Public Library Historic Photograph Collection.)

McKercher Bridge, which replaced an earlier covered span at the same site, was built by Linn County in 1932 following the standard state plans. The costs to build the 105-foot Howe truss totaled $5,893.10. In 1940, the inspector noted that the camber in the truss needed to be adjusted and that the bridge needed to be painted. In 1956, the inspector stated, "Recommend to Bridge Dep't this structure be placed on an early program for replacement." (Courtesy ODOT.)

The Wiley Creek Bridge, also known as Old Foster Bridge, was built in 1917. The 83-foot Howe truss span was located a short distance from the Foster Post Office. The town has since been relocated. Linn County expended $1,400 in construction costs. Overhead clearance was 13 feet 8 inches. The 1943 inspector's report stated, "This structure to be reinforced or replaced in two or three years." The bridge was closed to traffic and survived into the 1950s before it was dismantled. (Courtesy ODOT.)

Linn County built the Hufford Bridge in 1938 following state-approved engineering plans. The one-span Howe truss bridge measured 120 feet over the Middle Fork of the Santiam River. Construction costs totaled $6,500. The bridge enjoyed a short life of just 28 years before being dynamited for the new lake in 1966. (Courtesy ODOT.)

The 90-foot Howe truss Hoffman Bridge was built by Linn County in 1936. Gothic-style windows were installed into the housing instead of open sides. The upper and lower chords are hand-hewn Douglas fir logs, and visitors can see the adze marks on these timbers. The oval portals were enlarged for bus and truck traffic in 1974. (Courtesy ODOT.)

Just a mile east of McKercher Bridge, the Crawfordsville Bridge spans the Calapooia River near the edge of town. Linn County workers built the 105-foot Howe truss bridge in 1932. A continuous window on each side helps provide light and ventilate the covered span. A new concrete bridge replaced it in 1962, and the Crawfordsville Bridge has since been transferred to the parks department. (Courtesy ODOT.)

U. B. Peters Bridge was one of the Albany Ditch covered spans. The 60-foot Howe truss structure was built near Albany in 1925 at a cost of $1,845. Because it crossed the stream on a curve, one side was open, exposing the truss members. The little bridge lasted into the 1950s. (Courtesy ODOT.)

Built in 1928, Spring Creek Bridge was an 82-foot Howe truss span located three miles south of Harrisburg over Spring Creek. It cost the county about $1,900 to construct. The exact date of replacement is unknown, but the 1943 inspection reported the bridge at 70 percent. Also noted was that most of the water was overflow from the Willamette River. (Courtesy ODOT.)

This Albany Ditch bridge, known as the Talmon Bridge, was built in 1923 for just $600. The image implies it was 43 feet in length; however, the files at the Oregon Department of Transportation show the bridge was actually a 42-foot-9-inch queenpost truss. It lasted into the 1950s. (Courtesy ODOT.)

Sodom Ditch Bridge was another of Linn County's unadorned covered bridges. The 57-foot-4-inch Howe truss span included an overhead clearance of 13 feet 8 inches. The bridge survived into the 1950s. (Courtesy ODOT.)

Not far from the small community of Holley in eastern Linn County, Dollar Camp Bridge spanned the Calapooia River. Small traffic jams occurred at the 110-foot Howe truss structure, as traffic leaving the bridge had to stop for the trains traveling past. The bridge was replaced in 1951. (Courtesy ODOT.)

Farther up the Calapooia River from the Dollar Camp Bridge was this covered span, supported by an 82-foot Howe truss. Built in 1926, the bridge was modeled in the old Linn County construction style and lasted into the 1950s. (Courtesy ODOT.)

The first Bohemian Hall Covered Bridge was constructed about 100 yards east of its replacement and spanned Crabtree Creek in an east-west direction, not the north-south direction of the second. This bridge was a 132-foot Howe truss built sometime between 1905 and 1910. The 1943 inspection report noted that the roof had been removed and that the truss camber needed to be corrected. It also stated that an alternate bridge was needed soon, because the truss was only 50 percent good. The span was replaced in 1947. (Courtesy ODOT.)

Taken by the author in 1975, this photograph shows the second Bohemian Hall Bridge, which spanned Crabtree Creek at its site on Richardson Gap Road. This bridge, built in 1947, was a 120-foot Howe truss structure housed entirely in corrugated sheet metal. It was removed from service in 1987. The timbers were to be used in rebuilding the bridge at another site; however, dry rot and decay made them unusable.

Linn Co – Crabtree Creek – 105'sp. 1939

6-12876

Larwood Bridge was constructed in 1939 to replace an existing covered bridge that had been built prior to 1900. The bridge pictured here was built following the authorized state engineering plans, along with a Linn County modification to allow open sides in the housing. Building costs of the 105-foot Howe truss structure totaled about $7,000. (Courtesy ODOT.)

Linn Co – Thomas Cr. 90'sp. 1937

2-12958

One of several roofed structures to cross Thomas Creek, Jordan Bridge was built in 1937 at a cost of $1,850. It was a six-panel, 90-foot Howe truss span. By 1980, Linn County was considering replacing the roofed bridge, and in 1985, it was dismantled and the pieces marked for rebuilding. The timbers were trucked to Stayton in Marion County, where the Jordan Bridge was rebuilt in Pioneer Park. It burned in 1994 but was again re-created in 1998. (Courtesy ODOT.)

Shimanek Bridge was the second or third covered bridge at this site. Built in 1927 (not 1937, as the photograph shows), it was a 130-foot Howe truss with wooden piers. The bridge was severely damaged in the 1962 Columbus Day windstorm. (Courtesy ODOT.)

This photograph, taken in 1963, reveals the damaged Shimanek Bridge. It was completely rebuilt in 1966. (Courtesy Salem Public Library Historic Photograph Collection.)

Short Bridge spanned the South Santiam River near Cascadia on High Deck Road. The county built this 116-foot Howe truss in 1925 for $1,550. Its replacement was completed in 1945. The 1943 inspection report stated, "Truss in bad shape. Rotten chords and floor beams but heavily loaded log trucks are using structure continuously." (Courtesy ODOT.)

Bryant Park Bridge passed over the Calapooia River at the entrance of Bryant Park in Albany. The rustic-looking structure displayed a covered pedestrian walkway, a rarity in Oregon covered bridges. The 130-foot Howe truss span was built in 1924 and lasted until 1962, when it gave way to a concrete bridge. (Courtesy ODOT.)

Weddle Bridge crossed Thomas Creek near Scio until it was dismantled. The timbers were moved to Sweet Home's Sanky Park and the bridge rebuilt. This photograph, taken by the author in 1987, shows the Weddle Bridge at its original location. Linn County built this 120-foot Howe truss bridge in 1937 for $2,450. Weddle Bridge replaced an earlier covered bridge at the same Thomas Creek site.

Bates Park Bridge consisted of two separate spans, each built at a different time. The older red span was a 139-foot-6-inch length built in 1921 and replaced in 1957. The white bridge, measuring 153 feet 8 inches long, was constructed in 1930 and replaced in 1970. Bates Park Bridge crossed the Santiam River near Lebanon. (Courtesy ODOT.)

The 48-foot Beaver Creek Bridge spanned the stream near Crabtree in Linn County. Several bents under the floor beams supported the old bridge during its last years of service. Siding boards were removed to reduce the dead weight. The bridge was replaced when road realignment was performed in 1940. (Courtesy ODOT.)

This covered bridge over Murder Creek was built three miles north of Albany on the old Pacific Highway in 1905. The 72-foot truss was designed in the old Linn County style. In 1922, it was replaced with a concrete span. (Courtesy ODOT.)

Ten

MARION AND POLK COUNTIES

The 100-foot Howe truss McKee Bridge crossed the Pudding River north of Mount Angel. It was built for Marion County in 1907 and lasted until 1949, when it was replaced with a steel truss bridge. Both Marion and Polk Counties constructed covered bridges, though they were rarely impressive in design. According to one historian, most were nothing more than a shed over water with openings at each end. Many bridges were left unpainted after completion. The Willamette River provides the dividing line between the two counties, yet no covered bridge was ever built to connect them. Today a small river ferry still plies the waters between the counties. More than 30 covered bridge sites have been found in Marion County. More than 20 have been documented in Polk County. Now just two covered bridges stand in Marion, and only one is left in Polk. (Courtesy ODOT.)

In 1935, Marion County built this Abiqua Creek covered bridge (No. 5443), a 70-foot Howe truss span at milepost 13.8 on Road 616, about seven miles southeast of Silverton. Construction costs totaled $2,600. The bridge was replaced in the 1950s. (Courtesy ODOT.)

Gallon House Bridge spans Abiqua Creek between the towns of Silverton and Mount Angel. A gallon house, which sold liquor by the quart and gallon, actually stood on the Mount Angel end in the early 1900s. The bridge, built in 1916, is an 84-foot Howe truss structure. It survived the 1964 flood, though with considerable damage. A complete rehabilitation in 1990 ensures the bridge will continue to serve Marion County travelers. (Courtesy ODOT.)

118

This 1943 inspector's photograph shows the Easson Bridge in its rural setting in Marion County near Mount Angel. This old wooden bridge, crossing the Pudding River, was built in 1912 as a 75-foot Howe truss span. Marion County paid $5,000 in construction costs. The bridge was replaced in the 1940s. (Courtesy ODOT.)

Often called the Prison Annex Bridge, Hobson Bridge in Marion County spanned Mill Creek about three miles east of Salem near the prison annex. The date of construction is not known. This 1946 view displays the dilapidated bridge one year before it was destroyed. (Courtesy Salem Public Library Historic Photograph Collection.)

Scotts Mills Bridge, also known as Newlen Bridge, crossed Butte Creek on the Clackamas and Marion line in the small logging community of Scotts Mills. Though the bridge was built in 1924, this 1936 photograph shows the bridge already in a weakened condition. It was replaced in 1951, when only five roofed bridges remained in Marion County. (Courtesy Salem Public Library Historic Photograph Collection.)

Pictured here is Salem's covered bridge during the 1890 flood. The old structure spanned South Mill Creek on Commercial Street. Dan Clarke and L. W. Hayden built the 200-foot wooden bridge in 1862 at a cost of $7,000. It was replaced soon after this photograph. Kinney Flour Mill is at the left. (Courtesy Salem Public Library Historic Photograph Collection.)

This 78-foot Howe truss structure, known as Jack's Bridge, passed over Butte Creek on the Marion and Clackamas line near Scotts Mills. Construction and maintenance costs were shared between the two counties. The bridge was replaced in the 1950s. (Courtesy Kildow collection.)

Seen during construction in 1881, this covered bridge spanned the North Santiam River at Mehama. The other span in this bridge was an iron truss. A devastating flood in 1890 washed it away. (Courtesy Kildow collection.)

The Gates Bridge was built in 1903 to span the North Santiam River near the small community of Gates. The 174-foot wooden bridge, located on the Marion and Linn line, lasted until its replacement in 1940. (Courtesy Kildow collection.)

The Blair Bridge, crossing Mill Creek near Buell, typified early Polk County features of bridge design. This structure was built in 1906 (not 1910, as the writing on the photograph shows) at a cost of just $714. It operated until the late 1940s. Shingled roofs, narrow daylight strips, board and batten siding, and wooden pilings were construction specifications required by the court. Sometimes a coat of paint was included, but most often it was not. (Courtesy ODOT.)

In 1919, Earl C. Bushnell built the 115-foot Wallace Bridge over the South Yamhill River between Buell and Valley Junction in Polk County. Bushnell used timbers 120 feet in length for the bottom chords. Years after construction, 12 windows were added to each side. Wallace Bridge was bypassed in 1935 but was left standing. Strong winds blew it into the river in the late 1940s. (Courtesy ODOT.)

Polk Co. — Luckiamute River — 100' span — 1906 /023

Just a short distance from the small community of Pedee, the old Ira Hooker Bridge spanned the Luckiamute River. The rustic-looking structure was a 100-foot housed span. According to county records, it was constructed in 1906. Siding boards without battens, a shingled roof, and wooden pilings for piers were common building features. The bridge was replaced in the 1940s. (Courtesy ODOT.)

Polk Co. — Luckiamute River 100' span 1906   10-232

This photograph gives an end view of the Ira Hooker Bridge over the Luckiamute River. A concrete bridge now spans the river at this spot. (Courtesy ODOT.)

The Dallas Water Works built this structure across Rickreall Creek in 1916. The 84-foot Howe truss bridge included exterior stabilizing buttresses. Corrugated metal provided the covering for the sides and roof. According to Ray Boydston, a retired employee of the water company, the construction costs were less than $1,000. The bridge collapsed in a winter storm in 1986.

Otis Hamar, a noted bridge builder in Polk and Lincoln Counties, constructed the Ritner Creek Bridge in 1927. The 75-foot Howe truss span cost Polk County $6,963.78. The bridge served on the secondary state highway until it was moved about 60 feet downstream and replaced with a concrete bridge in 1976. Rehabilitation was completed in 2007, restoring the bridge to its original look. (Courtesy ODOT.)

Bridgeport Bridge spanned the Luckiamute River a short distance from Falls City and five miles from Dallas. The 72-foot Howe truss structure was located on Highway 223. Also known as White Bridge, it was replaced in 1950. (Courtesy Salem Public Library Historic Photograph Collection.)

Although little is known about this bridge, it deserves mention here. It spanned Rickreall Creek near the small farm community, surviving until replacement in the early 1900s. (Courtesy Kildow collection.)

In 1895, contractors St. John and Stone built the Hagood Bridge at North Main Street over La Creole Creek (later renamed Rickreall Creek), one of the two covered bridges in Dallas. A concrete replacement eliminated this covered bridge in 1921. (Courtesy Oregon Historical Society.)

Visit us at
arcadiapublishing.com
··